THE
GARDENS
AT CASTLE
HOWARD

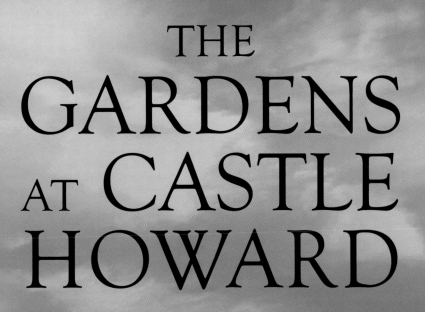

THE GARDENS AT CASTLE HOWARD

Mike Kipling

Introduction by Christopher Ridgway
Foreword by the Hon. Simon Howard

Frances Lincoln Limited
4 Torriano Mews
Torriano Avenue
London NW5 2RZ
www.franceslincoln.com

First Frances Lincoln edition 2010

A catalogue record for this book is available
from the British Library.

ISBN 9780711231436

Printed and bound in China

9 8 7 6 5 4 3 2 1

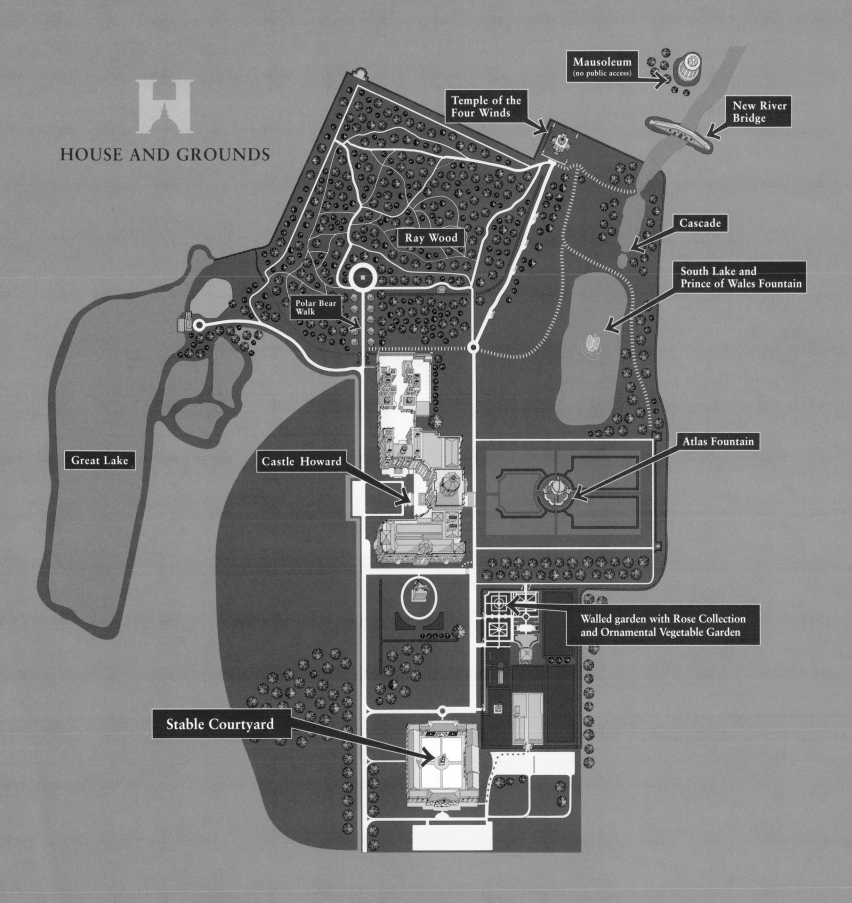

HOUSE AND GROUNDS

Mausoleum
(no public access)

Temple of the
Four Winds

New River
Bridge

Cascade

South Lake and
Prince of Wales Fountain

Ray Wood

Polar Bear
Walk

Atlas Fountain

Great Lake

Castle Howard

Walled garden with Rose Collection
and Ornamental Vegetable Garden

Stable Courtyard

CONTENTS

FOREWORD

One aspect of Castle Howard that not many give a thought to is the sheer volume of photographs that have been taken of the house and gardens. They vary from the sublime to the ridiculous!

The joy of Mike Kipling's superb book is that he takes us on a much deeper and more satisfying journey than the one-off 'good shot' most of us can manage with the help of a modern camera and a sunny day.

Through his superb photography he manages to tell the story of our home and estate through the changing seasons. It was a great personal pleasure to see that this book ventures further than the archetypal image of the façade of Castle Howard. Yes, the house in all its splendour is captured — as it must be in such a publication — but there's every other facet from humble vegetable gardens right through to the temple, mausoleum and fountains.

My wife and I are forever telling friends and visitors how Castle Howard is about so much more than the summer season. That there are several layers, as the seasons change, to the beautiful countryside that surrounds us. Mike Kipling has succeeded in capturing the very essence of the landscape and I sincerely hope this collection of work will encourage people to develop a year-long relationship with Castle Howard rather than simply an exclusively summer one.

It is testament to Mike Kipling that there wasn't a moment's hesitation in giving him absolute access to Castle Howard and the estate. He is the most unassuming of gentlemen and it's a great credit to him that he managed to spend a year in our 'back garden' without us ever really knowing he was there!

Simon Howard

CASTLE HOWARD

The landscape of Castle Howard has always been characterized by change of many kinds, from the dramatic transformation that accompanies the arrival of each season to the repeated refashioning of the terrain during the three centuries since it was first laid out in the early eighteenth century; today there are even moments when the gardens change on a day-to-day basis, as a hedge is clipped or a tree felled, or when big events are staged at Castle Howard and the grounds are strangely altered by all the accoutrements of mass entertainment. Yet were Charles Howard, 3rd Earl of Carlisle (1669–1738), the man responsible for the creation of this heroic landscape, to emerge from a time machine today he would still recognize the surroundings of his magnificent Baroque mansion. The landscape bears witness to alterations in the eighteenth, nineteenth and twentieth centuries, and even in the brief span of the third millennium it has already experienced further alteration in the form of improvement and restoration. Yet, in spite of generations of family intervention, much remains intact. In that respect it would be truer to say that the landscape of Castle Howard has been characterized by a balance of continuity and change: it is not a landscape frozen in the past, but nor has it abandoned that past.

While this dynamic of change means that Castle Howard has to be understood through time, its greatest appeal lies in the sheer scale of the terrain. To walk through the landscape here is to experience a multitude of sensations. The feet measure the physical distance; the eyes focus on things near or far; there are subtle smells in the atmosphere all year round; there are the sounds of wildlife, running water and wind in the trees; and even the silence at Castle Howard seems to have a special quality.

However, Castle Howard's magnificence is not simply due to the scale of the landscape, as an early visitor perceptively understood. John Tracy Atkyns was a law reporter renowned for taking correct notes in court, so there is no reason to doubt his word when towards the end of his lengthy tour of the house and grounds in 1732 he remarked: 'In short the chief excellency of these gardens consists in the infinite variety you see in them, so that you may very properly call it not one but ten different gardens.' A little later Atkyns became even more effusive, concluding, 'I don't pay it too great a compliment when I say that if our first parents, after being turned out of the Garden of Eden,

A double-flowered white cherry blossoming in May at the far end of the South Parterre.

William Aikman, *Charles Howard, 3rd Earl of Carlisle (1669–1738)*, painted 1728.

had been immediately placed upon this spot of ground, they would have concluded that they had only exchanged one Paradise for another.' Visitors today will appreciate Atkyns's sentiments. You can encounter lawns and parterres, a walled garden, rose gardens, herbaceous borders, hedges, a potager, terraces, woodlands, lakes and fountains, as well as grand, sweeping views with mysterious monuments in the distance that beckon to the viewer. You can move through a succession of outdoor spaces, each one in effect an individual garden. That is why Castle Howard never fails to satisfy: just like the splendid interiors with their magnificent collections, the grounds outside offer an embarrassment of riches. Anyone can enjoy these, whatever their interest: horticulturists, architectural enthusiasts, arboriculturists, painters, photographers, those who just enjoy walking and many who simply like to surrender to whatever is in front of them — all are as likely to depart in a state of enthusiasm as did John Tracy Atykns nearly three centuries ago.

So how did this landscape come into being? In 1698, as his political career began to shine, the 3rd Earl took the momentous decision to build for himself a mansion in this corner of Yorkshire in the parish of Henderskelfe. Close to the prosperous and important city of York, yet not too distant from London, which could be reached by coach in three or four days, the location was ideal for his needs. So he took a lease on the lands from his grandmother. As is well known, his masterstroke was to employ as his architect John Vanbrugh, a man who had never built anything in his life before; in turn Vanbrugh's most inspired move was to recruit Nicholas Hawksmoor to assist him, a man not only well experienced in the practicalities of building but an architect of genius in his own right. Thus Castle Howard was built by three men: the 3rd Earl of Carlisle, John Vanbrugh and Nicholas Hawksmoor. This talented triumvirate was responsible for not only the magnificent house but also the grounds, which included an astonishing array of monuments.

The single most important decision in terms of the construction of the house and its relationship to the landscape was its orientation.

Hendrik De Cort, *View of Castle Howard from the South East*, 1800.

Early proposals, before Vanbrugh became involved, showed a building that faced east—west. Vanbrugh rotated the house to face north—south, and this was to have enormous consequences with regard to the development of the gardens.

The building work began in 1699 and within fifteen years three-quarters of the house was finished and inhabited; all that remained to be built was the west wing. Despite Vanbrugh's urgent appeals to the 3rd Earl of Carlisle this was not begun until the 1750s, when it was completed by Sir Thomas Robinson under the direction of the 4th Earl. There are various reasons why the house was never fully finished in the lifetimes of the 3rd Earl, Vanbrugh and Hawksmoor, but perhaps the most significant is that after about 1715 Carlisle diverted nearly all his energy and funds into a hugely ambitious fashioning of the landscape.

The construction of Castle Howard was paralleled by a process of demolition, as its predecessor on the site, the medieval Henderskelfe Castle, along with the surrounding village and church, was flattened to make way for the new mansion and its cultivated surroundings. Today the only trace of the village that remains is the terrace that leads south-east from the house to the Temple of the Four Winds, following the route of the old main street.

Early on Carlisle was offered a set of garden proposals. These were attributed to George London, nurseryman and leading garden designer of the day, who is renowned for his formal garden designs with intricate ornamentation and geometry — a style that owed much to prevailing French and Dutch influences. But Carlisle accepted none of these early designs. He favoured a more innovative garden layout, and experimented with the surrounding landscape

in different ways. Before long contemporaries were unanimously praising the gardens and grounds for ushering in a new and more natural kind of gardening very different from that influenced by Continental styles.

It is to Ray Wood that we must look for evidence of a revolution in taste, as this ancient wood was transformed in these early years of the eighteenth century into an exciting woodland garden filled with architectural and sculptural features. Clearly one of the reasons why Ray Wood was the first area to be developed was that it was removed from the immediate vicinity of the new mansion which, for several years, was nothing more than a large construction site. Inside the wood Carlisle laid out a mazy and irregular network of paths, praised by one contemporary as a 'Labyrinth diverting model'. Indeed these pathways were so intricate that there was a famous

incident when members of the Howard family themselves became lost in the wood. The entrance piers were erected in 1705, and in the same year eight pedestals were positioned in the wood. Shortly afterwards lead sculptures were placed on them; and by 1710 'ye New Gardin in Ray Wood', as it was known, was filled with an extraordinary profusion of sculpture. Among the many statues were figures of Bacchus, Apollo, Neptune, a satyr, and a shepherd and his dog. Within ten to twenty years a host of figures would populate other parts of the grounds too. In 1723 the carver Andrew Carpenter is known to have supplied Carlisle with four lead figures: a Farnese Hercules, a Spartan boy, a faun, and a crouching Venus.

One of the most impressive pieces in Ray Wood, dating from this period, is a figure of Apollo, and in particular the ornate pedestal on which he stands, carved by the Huguenot craftsman Henri

The house, seen from the shadow of the avenue to the south-west, which was planted with lime trees and cedars in the nineteenth century.

Nadauld. Today this piece is sited at the end of the Lime Walk to the south of the house, having been moved there in the nineteenth century. The pedestal elicited great admiration from early visitors, on account of its detailed carving. In 1710 Thomas Player noted the Apollo 'on one of the pleasantest Rocks in the world'. Atkyns, in 1732, was more fulsome in his description: he declared it 'one of the prettiest things I ever saw, the basis at a distance seems a rude heap of stone but when you come nearer you may see in it, all the variety of prospect that the country can afford, villages, rocks, mountains, cataracts of water rolling down, and everything that can be beautiful in a landscape, carved on each side of it'. Today, in spite of the algae, the detail is still visible.

Also within the wood were numerous other architectural and sculptural features including a greenhouse, and summerhouses that were made of wood but painted to look like stone; there were seats, vases and two fountains, one with a figure of Neptune in the centre and a second with a carved swan at the top that spouted jets of water. There was also an amphitheatre, and a reservoir able to feed large streams of water that fell 'down 50 or 60 steps' before snaking out of sight. Early visitors' accounts record the diversity of mazy pathways in the wood, which terminated with various sights and views. Taken together, all these features – sculpture, buildings, waterworks – would have combined to present a theatre of incident in the wood. Each turn of the serpentine paths would have presented

a new spectacle, generating surprising or familiar sights, depending on which route one took.

By the 1720s Carlisle was expanding his landscaping schemes to include two temples on the edge of Ray Wood. One was Vanbrugh's Temple of Diana, located at the south-east corner of the wood and dating from the 1720s; nowadays this is known as the Temple of the Four Winds. Carlisle chose Vanbrugh's temple over a competing design by Hawksmoor, but ten years later Hawksmoor was granted an opportunity to build his own temple for the 3rd Earl: the Temple of Venus, dating from the early 1730s. Early photographs of about 1900 show this to have been an open rotunda with eight columns, with a heavy entablature and chunky lead-lined cap on top. The weight of this superstructure was clearly enormous, and as the stone decayed because of rusting iron cramps and damage by water and frost, the structure became less and less stable. By the 1930s the statue of Venus and her pedestal had been removed and relocated inside the Walled Gardens, and the Temple was shored up with timber. A few years later it was demolished as a dangerous structure; only the base remains today.

Further afield other buildings in the landscape included the first of the mock fortifications along the Avenue: the Carrmire Gate by Hawksmoor, dating from the late 1720s, with its gothic crenellations, arrowhead pinnacles and polygonal end turrets. The Carrmire Gate serves as a prelude to Vanbrugh's Pyramid Gatehouse 1 mile/1.6 kilometres further along the Avenue, erected in 1718, initially as the Pyramid Arch; the wings were added later, in 1756–8. Stretching out either side of the gatehouse, for half a mile/0.8 kilometres, are the Mock Fortifications, begun c.1720. These recall not just the medieval walls of the city of Chester (Vanbrugh's early home town) but also those of the nearby city of York, as well as the walls of ancient Rome, punctuated as they were by turrets, towers, bastions and pyramids. Hawksmoor was to extend this Romano-Egyptian

William Marlow, *A View of Castle Howard, the South Front*, c.1770.

motif to the east along the same ridge as the gatehouse with his large Pyramid of 1728. Set on a low plinth and flanked by four pairs of angled piers, acting almost like sentinels, the Pyramid is hollow, and contains a bust of the 3rd Earl's great-great-great grandfather, Lord William Howard.

And at the head of the drive, was the Obelisk, erected in 1714 by Vanbrugh, perhaps only the second to be built in eighteenth-century England (after Hawksmoor's obelisk in Ripon marketplace). Two sets of inscriptions were added in 1731, one commemorating the victories of the Duke of Marlborough, the other memorializing Carlisle's architectural achievements and dynastic aspirations.

Beginning to take shape at this time too was the 5 mile/8 kilometre-long approach to Castle Howard known as the Avenue, its plantations dating from 1704. Many of these trees, when mature, were lost in a violent storm in January 1839, when nearly 2,000 trees were blown down. Many of the mature lime trees in the Avenue today are part of the replanting that followed.

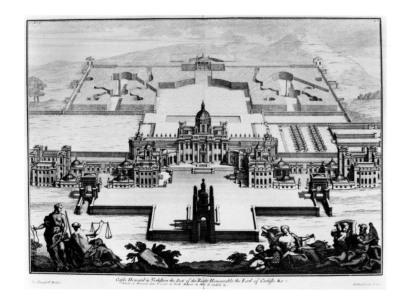

Bird's-eye view of Castle Howard from *Vitruvius Britannicus*, 1725.

The final structure in the landscape from this spectacular early phase of building was of course the grandest monument of them all: Hawksmoor's Mausoleum, begun in 1729. During the 1720s Carlisle had declared his wish to build a burial place for himself and his family; following Vanbrugh's death in 1726 Hawksmoor was entrusted with bringing this project to fruition.

Carlisle's wealth and energy, and his fruitful collaboration with Vanbrugh and Hawksmoor in the first three decades of the eighteenth century, resulted in the complete transformation of the landscape. Gone were the medieval castle, houses, church and network of agricultural smallholdings that comprised the village of Henderskelfe. In their place there emerged a landscape fashioned on an heroic scale. At the heart of this enterprise lay the mansion with its unique crowning dome, itself a masterpiece of Baroque design: Carlisle's home and also his palace, as seen in the famous bird's-eye view in *Vitruvius Britannicus* in 1725.

An estate map of 1727 illustrates the gardens immediately behind the house, where Vanbrugh had laid out a grass parterre filled with obelisks, vases, statues and a large Ionic column. When the artist William Marlow painted the parterre at the end of the eighteenth century the obelisks and vases had been removed and an expanse of lawn ran right up to the house. All that remained was the Ionic pillar, and the two sculptural groups on big composite pedestals designed by Hawksmoor: Hercules Wrestling with Antaeus, and Pluto and Proserpine. These groups disappeared at the end of the nineteenth century, but were rebuilt at the beginning of the twenty-first century as the culmination of a restoration programme that treated all the lead sculptures in the grounds.

The 1727 map also depicts a walled garden to the south-west of the house. This area was entered through the Satyr Gate, which was ornamented by two sets of vigorously carved heads and flower baskets, all executed by the Yorkshire carver Samuel Carpenter in 1705. Later in the century the Walled Garden was enlarged: heated walls, hot houses and a conservatory were installed, allowing vines,

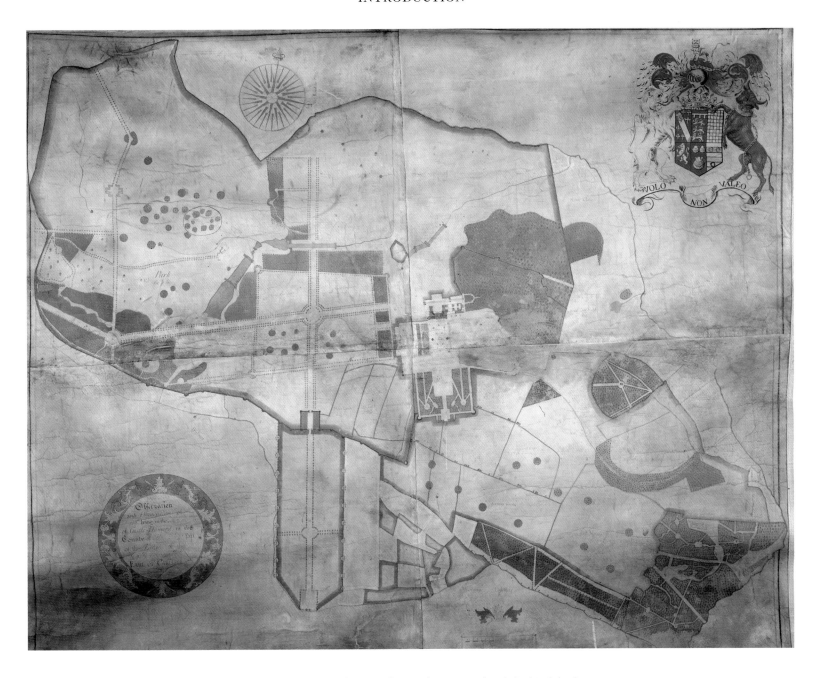

An estate map of 1727, showing the gardens immediately behind the house.

citrus fruits and even pomegranates to be grown. These buildings were refashioned in the nineteenth century, but today nothing remains of them, although the flues in the walls are visible.

Further afield the map of 1727 also reveals how the mansion was surrounded by a medley of buildings, each with a different architectural lineage — gothic walls and turrets, Roman temples, towers and arches, Egyptian pyramids; it was almost as if Carlisle had decided to assemble the history of European architecture in his back garden. This architectural largesse was matched by a huge

programme of tree planting, which signalled a desire to marry sound husbandry with a confident eye on posterity; after all, it takes an act of faith to plant a tree knowing that one will not see it come to full maturity, while the commercial value of this timber, climaxing a hundred years or so later, would be of great importance to his descendants.

By the time of his death in 1738 Carlisle had, with the exception of the unfinished west wing of the house, completed his grand project. What began as a way of enhancing his political and public

status had soon changed into a private project once he had lost political office and retired to Yorkshire, away from public life. He succeeded in raising the most comprehensive monument possible: Castle Howard was an entire landscape fashioned in his name, which would dwarf the ephemeral glories of political life and last well beyond his own lifetime. In this respect it was perhaps fitting that the grandest monument in the landscape, the Mausoleum, should take its meaning from human mortality: it was through the cycle of death and the birth of successive generations that Castle Howard endured.

But all landscape is subject to change, and while the core identity of Castle Howard remained untouched, as the decades passed there were pockets of alteration. By the 1770s many of the features in Ray Wood had vanished: the paths seem to have fallen into decay, the statues were removed and the sophisticated waterworks dismantled. No traces of these remain, apart from the circular reservoir at the top of the hill, which holds over half a million gallons/quarter of a million litres. A basin of some sort has been sited in the wood since the early eighteenth century, but the present version was rebuilt in the late 1840s, although it is likely that the pedestal in the centre dates from earlier. The base of the pedestal reveals, when the pool is empty, a series of carved creatures on one face only. Why they should be there is a mystery, especially as they are concealed beneath the waterline for most of the time.

After the South Lake had been completed, early in the 1730s, it was decided to open up the waterways beyond it with the construction of a serpentine river that flowed in a south-easterly direction before disappearing into a wood. An eighteenth-century plan shows clearly the curved bastion wall or dam at the end of the South Lake and, beyond, the course of New River, with the bridge that spans it, built in the 1740s and designed as a frame to the Mausoleum on the hill above.

The Atlas Fountain plays its jets in spite of the cold weather, as the late afternoon December sun warms the stone of the house.

William Nesfield's embroidered parterre to the south of the house, with the Atlas Fountain as the centrepiece. Laid out in the early 1850s, the parterre was removed at the end of the nineteenth century, but the fountain was retained.

During the time of the 5th Earl (1748–1825) the most important development was the creation of the Great Lake to the north of the house. As early as the 1720s Hawksmoor had suggested to the 3rd Earl that an area of boggy ground with a few fishponds could be transformed into a spectacular lake, with the village of Coneysthorpe on the far side. But it was not until 1796 that this area was embanked and flooded to create a new 'sheet of water' covering nearly 80 acres/32 hectares. At the same time the pond on the southern shore, closest to the house, was created and named Dairy Pond on account of its proximity to the model dairies built by the 5th Earl.

By the close of the century Castle Howard remained largely an early eighteenth-century landscape. After the efforts of the 3rd Earl, and his son the 4th Earl (1694–1758), who oversaw the completion of the house and the Mausoleum, Castle Howard seems, miraculously, to have been ignored and largely left alone. Thus Capability Brown never came to Castle Howard; nor did Humphry Repton. There was no desire on the part of later generations to improve the grounds in the way that so many owners did elsewhere in England between 1770 and 1830.

All this was to change, however, in the nineteenth century with the arrival at Castle Howard of the great Victorian landscape gardener William Andrews Nesfield. Consulted or commissioned at estates all across Britain, Nesfield was, from 1840 to 1860, the premier landscape gardener in the country. His main work at Castle Howard dates from 1850, when the 7th Earl commissioned him to create an ornamental parterre to the south of the house, where previously there had been an expanse of lawn, and to build two grand fountains: the Atlas Fountain and a second fountain for the South Lake, known as the Prince of Wales Fountain.

The installation of Nesfield's fountains and parterre entailed huge costs: his initial estimate of £2,000 proved wildly inaccurate and the total expenditure after five years of work was a staggering £10,000. Notwithstanding these financial strains, a decade later a second phase of improvements was begun, developing the vista towards New River Bridge and the Mausoleum, and extending the South Waterways. Prompted by a watercolour view he had painted a few years before, Nesfield advised on the construction of the Cascade, Temple Hole Basin and the Waterfall, thus linking the South Lake with New River beyond.

One of Nesfield's principal aims was to exploit the vista between the house and the Mausoleum, and a photograph taken during the 1870s reveals how successfully he achieved this, with a broad view from the house across the South Lake to New River Bridge and the Mausoleum. In fact the vista was also conceived in terms of the reciprocal view, from the Mausoleum to the house. But the *tromp-l'oeil* effect from the house is impressive, with the illusion of an almost continuous and level sheet of water between the South Lake and New River Bridge, when there is in fact a drop of nearly 40 feet/12 metres.

Within forty years of its completion, in the 1890s, much of Nesfield's landscaping was swept away by Rosalind Howard, 9th Countess of Carlisle. She replaced the ornamental parterre on the South Front with the grass terraces and yew hedges visible today. From their earliest visits to Castle Howard both the Countess and her husband were alarmed by the costs of maintaining the gardens, especially at the expense of improving the tenant farms. Thus her erasure of Nesfield's parterre and her alterations to the lake were prompted in part by aesthetic considerations, but also as a way of

The fire of 9 November 1940 destroyed twenty rooms and the famous dome, which was rebuilt in 1960. (Photograph © *Yorkshire Post*)

making economies. On the slopes above the South Lake she planted trees and shrubs, which would in time completely obscure the vista between the house and the Mausoleum.

The mid-twentieth century was a dark period for the family, the house and the estate. Two sons died in action in the Second World War, and in 1940 a fire decimated much of the building and its precious contents. In the grounds much of the landscape disappeared into obscurity, while on the north side of the house the shores of the Great Lake became silted up and overgrown. Some of the buildings became in danger of collapse, including Vanbrugh's temple and even the Mausoleum. But the story of the last sixty years has been one of restoration, both in the house and outdoors throughout the grounds.

The epic story of recovery began with George Howard (1920–1984), who returned from the war to discover that he was the unexpected heir to Castle Howard, and faced with the daunting task of owning and managing an estate that had suffered from years of neglect, as well as a mansion substantially damaged by fire. Many individuals would have walked away from such a challenge, but not George Howard. Resolving to keep Castle Howard as a family home, he and his wife, Lady Cecilia, courageously set about restoring the house and other buildings and in 1958 opened Castle Howard to the visiting public.

Among the first projects he embarked on was the restoration of Vanbrugh's temple, which was by now in a state of decay: the timbers were infested with dry rot and beetle damage, the stonework was badly eroded and the interiors were in poor condition. Between 1954 and 1956 the dome of the temple was completely rebuilt and the plasterwork inside renewed. Little did anyone realize that this project would mark the beginning of a programme of restoration and renewal that continued for the rest of the twentieth century. After rebuilding the dome on the house in the early 1960s, and so restoring Castle Howard's true architectural appearance and character, work focused once more on the outdoors. At the end of

the 1970s the Mausoleum was in urgent need of repair, and in a complex and enormously expensive project the entire colonnade was rebuilt. This involved dismantling each of the twenty Doric columns and rebuilding them with new stone; but unfortunately the funding did not extend to repairing the steps and entablature. Nevertheless the Mausoleum was made secure as a structure, and it continues to dominate the south-east vista across the South Lake.

Beginning in the 1980s the South Waterways were completely restored and recovered. The work was carried out in separate phases, starting with Ray Wood Reservoir, and followed by Nesfield's Atlas Fountain. The stonework for both structures was refurbished and their basins made fully watertight. Then in 1987 a major project was begun to restore the entire mile-long stretch of waterways beyond, linking the South Lake with the Cascade, Temple Hole Basin, the Waterfall and New River. The South Lake was drained and dredged, as were Temple Hole Basin and eventually New River. Their banks were cleared of excess vegetation and their shorelines redefined: the South Lake and Temple Hole Basin share something of the Victorian geometry as fashioned by Nesfield — a rectangle with quadrants at the corners — whereas the eighteenth-century New River has a serpentine shape. The stonework for the Cascade, Waterfall and New River Bridge was also repaired and where necessary replaced.

At the same time the Prince of Wales Fountain on the South Lake was refurbished. With the lake empty it was discovered that the pipes for the eight subsidiary jets surrounding the central spike — known as the feathers, because they resemble the feathers in the Prince of Wales's crest — had been bent flat on to the lake bed earlier in the century, and they were repositioned so that they could play correctly. The entire project has recovered a part of the landscape that had been shrouded by overgrown vegetation for decades. Today the fountains and waterways not only look spectacular but also sound very pleasing, with water splashing in fountains, cascades and waterfalls.

Portrait of George Howard by Trevor Stubley, 1981.

The Walled Garden to the south-west of the house had remained productive throughout the nineteenth and twentieth centuries, with areas devoted to flowers and, during wartime, growing vegetables; for a short while this area even supported a market garden programme. As the house grew in popularity as a visitor destination, however, the western section was turned into a plant centre, which has been expanded in recent years. In the 1970s sections of the Walled Garden at the eastern end were transformed into rose gardens, beginning in 1975 with Lady Cecilia's Garden, laid out by George Howard in memory of his wife. This was followed by the Sundial Garden in 1977, and the Venus Garden in 1979. These were designed by James Russell, who had moved to Castle Howard from Sunningdale Nurseries in the 1960s. In the early 1990s soil sickness was diagnosed in both the Sundial and Venus Gardens, so more than 40,000 cubic feet/1,132 cubic metres of soil had to be replaced and the gardens were replanted with modern roses. But such is the pace of change at Castle Howard that in 2004 the Sundial Garden was transformed once more, this time into a potager, an ornamental vegetable garden, specializing in old and new varieties of vegetables. Thus the area is beginning to recover some of its past identity as the major provider of fruit, vegetables, herbs and flowers for consumption in the house.

Just as the Walled Garden underwent rapid change in the last decades of the twentieth century, so too did other parts of the gardens. Ray Wood was clear-felled during the Second World War, and for years afterwards the hilltop to the east of the house remained bare and unplanted. In the 1960s George Howard and James Russell decided to reinstate some of the meandering pathways that had made the wood famous in the eighteenth century; at the same time the area was planted with native broadleaves, which in time would grow to give the wood a new canopy. Around this framework James Russell began to fill Ray Wood with new ornamental plantings, including nearly 800 species of rhododendron, as well as glades of pieris, wild roses, magnolias, hydrangeas, viburnums, maples and rowans. Many of these were grown from seed that he had gathered on expeditions to places around the world including the Himalayas, China, Japan, South Africa, New Zealand and South America. Clumps of bamboo provide shelter from the wind and Ray Wood contains many specimens once considered too tender to grow so far north in Yorkshire. Today the wood is jointly managed by Castle Howard and Kew Gardens, through the Castle Howard Arboretum Trust, which is also responsible for the Arboretum, another creation by James Russell, which lies on the western side of the estate.

Three hundred years after Castle Howard was built the house, landscape and estate remain as dynamic as ever. Disaster and decay in the twentieth century proved to be the prelude to heroic restoration and recovery both indoors and outdoors. Not only have natural features been reclaimed from wilderness but buildings have been repaired and preserved. One of the most successful projects of recent times has been the restoration of all the lead sculptures in the grounds.

Herein lies the secret to Castle Howard: the constant cycle of change underpinned by continuity. The images here record a year in the landscape, and in the course of twelve months the forms and colours of all that is visible undergo frequent shifts and changes. No two visits are ever the same: on clear days in summer the detail and variety are brought into sharp focus, but on misty days in winter a dramatic atmosphere pervades the grounds. Castle Howard never stands still; it remains a landscape of perpetual drama and event.

SPRING

Spring is one of the most exciting periods in the Castle Howard calendar. The landscape awakes from the coldness of winter. Carpets of snowdrops are the first sign of this awakening in the Polar Bear Walk at the entrance to Ray Wood. Either by design or natural seeding, small clumps have also established themselves in woodland throughout the estate.

Following the snowdrops are the daffodils that are one of the many major delights of Castle Howard. The main plantings are alongside Ray Wood and the Stable Courtyard, although they are found in abundance all around the estate. Clever selection of species has ensured that the daffodil season is as long as possible.

Bluebells and other wild flowers such as primroses are establishing themselves in Ray Wood and their flowering heralds the beginning of the rhododendron and azalea season. Spread throughout Ray Wood, Temple Terrace and around the shores of South Lake, these are one of the best rhododendron and azalea collections in England.

A mixture of early and later daffodil varieties, some with short stems and others with long, guarantees continuous flowering from March until May.

LEFT Above the shores of the South Lake are plantings of brilliant red rhododendrons.

ABOVE Rhododendrons on the west side of the Temple Terrace.

Peacocks are a familiar sight at Castle Howard, strutting about the gardens and making a spectacular display of feathers, but curiously peahens never seem to settle in the grounds.

Snowdrops below the temple.

A sea of snowdrops on the edge of Ray Wood, with the Medici Vase behind them.

Each May the floor of Pretty Wood – to the south-east of Castle Howard – is carpeted with bluebells.

Rhododendron 'Hino Mayo' in Ray Wood. The world-famous plantings of azaleas and rhododendrons were begun by James Russell in 1975.

ABOVE The view west from the edge of Mount Sion Wood under glowering skies. The triple-arched New River Bridge, designed possibly by Daniel Garrett in the 1740s, spans New River, which was created a decade earlier. In the middle distance is Temple Rush Wood and beyond the south façade of the house.

RIGHT Wild garlic, otherwise known as ransoms, blooming alongside the Avenue in May.

STATUES

One of the most successful projects of recent times has been the restoration of all the lead sculptures in the grounds. Over the years these eighteenth-century figures had decayed, and because lead is a pliable metal, prone to distortion, it was not uncommon to see them propped up by poles or twisting out of shape. Between 1993 and 2001 each figure, some weighing as much 1½ tons, was removed from its pedestal and taken to a special workshop on the estate. There it was opened up and the old iron support inside the hollow figure, which had corroded badly, was removed and replaced by a stainless-steel armature to ensure that the statue retained its correct, upright posture. Cracks were repaired and missing bits replaced; in some cases, such as the Borghese Gladiator and the figure of Antinous, almost entire sections had to be cast anew. In previous centuries these figures had been painted white to mimic marble or stone, but today this practice is no longer observed, as lead is more widely appreciated for its own sake, and in any case a painted coating would make it harder to monitor the condition of the pieces. Eighteen life-size figures in the grounds have either been repaired or, in the case of Hercules and Antaeus, and Pluto and Proserpine, commissioned as brand-new compositions to replace missing ones. Today Castle Howard boasts one of the finest lead sculpture collections in the UK.

LEFT The Borghese Gladiator.

ABOVE A detail from one of the two large tazzas or planters on the South Parterre. These have been attributed to the architect Charles Heathcoate Tatham, who worked at Castle Howard between 1800 and 1810. The large acanthus leaf erupts into two big scrolls.

OPPOSITE, CLOCKWISE FROM TOP LEFT
Figure of the Greek hero Meleager, supplied by John Nost, *c.*1708. Accompanying Meleager is his
faithful hound, while his hand rests upon the head of the Calydonian boar which he had killed.

Bacchus, the first of the statues on the terrace leading to the temple, was part of a consignment of lead
sculptures purchased from the London yard of John Nost in the first decade of the eighteenth century.

The figure of Spinario was once said to represent a conscientious shepherd boy who was
entrusted to deliver a message to the Roman Senate and only stopped to remove a thorn from
his foot once he had delivered it. Supplied by Andrew Carpenter in 1723, the statue was
restored in 1995 and placed on a new pedestal carved with branches and leaves.

The Dancing Fawn has been located on the South Parterre ever since it was purchased in 1723.

The Farnese Hercules, so called on account of the ancient version in the Farnese Palace in Rome in the sixteenth
century, which spawned thousands of copies in marble, plaster and lead. Draped over his club is his cloak,
fashioned out of the hide of the Nemean lion, the killing of which was the first of Hercules' twelve labours.

Antinous, the beautiful youth with whom the Emperor Hadrian was said to have been infatuated.
When he drowned in the Nile, Hadrian ordered that he be deified.

ABOVE A marble copy of the famous Uffizi Boar in Florence, purchased by the 5th Earl during
his tour of Italy in 1768 for the price of 150 sequins. Sequins were gold coins minted in Italy.

ABOVE The western steps of the temple, with the figures of Crispina on the left and Mammea on the right. All four figures for the temple were supplied by Andrew Carpenter, *c.*1731.

RIGHT The figure of Mammea on the south-west pier of the Temple of the Four Winds.

SUMMER

In summer the trees are in full leaf, and the strong light and pronounced shade dramatize the landscape. The crisp early morning sunlight, blazing across the South Lake, highlights a wealth of architectural detail on the south façade. On long evenings the sinking sun illuminates the north façade, and provides spectacular views across the Great Lake to the house.

ABOVE The Medici Vase at the top of the slope into Ray Wood. Purchased by the 5th Earl in 1778, this is a Coade stone replica of the famous version in the Uffizi Gallery in Florence. It is decorated with figures thought to represent the sacrifice of Iphigenia by the Greeks to the goddess Diana at the outset of the Trojan War. The pedestal is decorated with three medallions and the poem in Latin records how Ray Wood is sacred to the memory of Diana, goddess of hunting and chastity. Coade stone was a ceramic material used as artificial stone; the process was pioneered by Mrs Eleanor Coade in her factory in London in the late 1760s.

RIGHT A classic view of the South Front from the south-west; in the foreground is one of the many eighteenth-century lead sculptures, with a peacock slinking by.

BELOW LEFT The South Front doorway, surrounded by carvings of heads wearing helmets and laurel leaves; the keystone is another mask (allegedly of the 3rd Earl of Carlisle), with a cartouche bearing the family cipher of interlinked Cs. The fluted pilasters either side of the doorway do not match those on the north side of the building. When challenged over this architectural solecism, Hawksmoor famously replied that nobody could see both fronts simultaneously!

BELOW RIGHT As the eye travels upwards the detail on the façade only seems to multiply, with urns and statues decorating the skyline, gigantic busts surrounding the dome and a gilded lantern that gleams on sunny days and can be seen for miles.

RIGHT Up these steps on the north side would arrive any important guest in the eighteenth century, to the doors leading into the spectacular Great Hall. The Doric pilasters (plain, unlike the fluted Corinthian ones on the south side) divide the façade into vertical bands, which are filled with a rich array of carved cherubs, trophies, masks and a frieze.

FOR YOUR OWN SAFETY
PLEASE KEEP OFF THE STEPS

To the north of the house the ground falls away, leading down to the Dairy Pond, fashioned in the eighteenth century. One of the famous black swans swims by.

LEFT TOP Had Castle Howard been finished by Vanbrugh,
it would have presented a completely symmetrical façade. Instead,
the east and west ends (seen here right and left) are materially different.

LEFT BOTTOM Castle Howard was built by Vanbrugh from east to west
(here left to right), and the west wing was intended to mirror the eastern
one exactly. But the 3rd Earl, Vanbrugh and Hawksmoor all died before
this wing was begun. It fell to the 4th Earl to complete the house, for
which he employed his brother-in-law, the amateur architect Sir Thomas
Robinson. His Palladian wing is at odds with the Baroque style of the
rest of Vanbrugh's building, and had he prevailed there is no doubt that
once he had finished the West Wing Robinson would have progressed
eastwards, tearing down Vanbrugh's house and replacing it with a wholly
new one. Fortunately the 4th Earl vetoed this proposal, and in his later
years he bitterly regretted his choice of Robinson as architect. Thus
today the two wings are mismatched; one eighteenth-century visitor
imagined them saying to one another, 'What are you doing here?'

ABOVE Sir Thomas Robinson's West Wing, begun in the 1750s and
finally completed in the first decade of the nineteenth century.
His shallow octagonal dome mimics Vanbrugh's original.

FOLLOWING PAGES The long sweep of water that is the South Lake leads
inexorably to the house, seen here above the lake's western shoreline.

THE WALLED GARDEN

At their best in the months of June, July and August, the Rose Gardens – Lady Cecilia's Garden, which George Howard laid out in 1975 in memory of his wife, and the Venus Garden created in 1979 – are a pleasure to look at and to wander through They are filled with a variety of roses, herbaceous plants and flowering shrubs, many of which give off delightful perfumed aromas. The pond is filled with carp, some a good 15 inches/35 centimetres long. The potager or ornamental vegetable garden, established in 2008 in the Sundial Garden, grows organic vegetables that are sold in the estate shop, and has proved to be immensely popular with young and old visitors alike.

LEFT The dipping pond in the Walled Garden, with the Gardener's House beyond.

ABOVE The water lilies in the dipping pond flower in June.

55

THE WALLED GARDEN

LEFT ABOVE The pergola in the Rose Garden runs
alongside the eastern wall of the Walled Garden.

LEFT BELOW A twentieth-century urn in front of a hornbeam arbour.

BELOW The pergola was made from Castle Howard oak
and supports 'Seagull' and 'Rambling Rector' roses.

FOLLOWING PAGES Lavender, *Campanula lactiflora*,
and *Rosa* 'Hebe's Lip' in Lady Cecilia's Garden.

ABOVE Delphinium borders in the Walled Garden, with begonias
inside the trimmed and patterned box hedging.

BELOW LEFT Over thirty varieties of delphinium flower every June and July.

BELOW RIGHT Water spouts from this lead mask and splashes on to the stone surface below, creating a curtain of water as it falls into the basin.

LEFT *Rosa* 'Armada', a modern shrub rose, in the Venus Garden.

ABOVE A white *Rosa* 'Madame Legras de St Germain' with yew
hedging, honeysuckle and a fuchsia border beyond.

FAR LEFT Florence fennel, harvested in July

LEFT Red 'Drumhead' cabbage, a hardy historic variety which may have been grown at Castle Howard in previous centuries.

BELOW The Castle Howard head gardener inspecting his pumpkins, behind a border of marigolds.

RIGHT Modern varieties of sweetcorn, 'Kite' F1, on the northern border of the potager.

A panoramic view of the potager in summer,
with the house in the distance.

THE TEMPLE OF THE FOUR WINDS

The Temple of the Four Winds owes its form to Italian antecedents, particularly Andrea Palladio's famous sixteenth-century Villa Almerico Capra at Vicenza, commonly known as the Villa Rotonda. The building is essentially a cube with a dome on top, and four Ionic tetrastyle porticoes, the pediments and corners above decorated with urns. The four lead statues of Roman empresses beside the steps on the east and west elevations were supplied by Andrew Carpenter in 1731. Unlike Palladio's original, which was a dwelling, Vanbrugh's temple was designed as a pavilion in which to take refreshment or to pursue leisure activities such as reading or sketching. The interior, decorated with scagliola by the Italian stuccoist Francesco Vassalli, was completed in 1739. Inside, busts of Roman emperors and empresses rest in circular niches above the doorways, the dome is decorated with gilded plasterwork and high inside the little lantern at the top are four gilded faces. Beneath the temple is a cellar where servants stored and prepared food and drink to serve to the polite company as they entertained above.

In the eighteenth century the Temple of the Four Winds, reached by the terrace from the house, would have marked the furthest extremity for polite society venturing outdoors on foot.

LEFT Aberdeen Angus cattle grazing in Carr Field to the east of Vanbrugh's temple. At Castle Howard the landscape of dressed lawns, sculpture and architectural delights has always co-existed with a working agricultural landscape.

ABOVE The eastern façade of the temple, with the steps that lead down into the parkland. In the eighteenth century it would have marked the route from the temple to the Mausoleum.

THE MAUSOLEUM

Hawksmoor's Mausoleum, begun in 1729 after Carlisle declared his wish to build a burial place for himself and his family, is the grandest monument in the Castle Howard landscape.

The correspondence between Carlisle and Hawksmoor for this period is full of references to buildings from the antique as possible models. Initially Hawksmoor based his design on the Tomb of Cecilia Metella in Rome; he envisaged a cylindrical drum and arcade, adding a clerestory above and a smaller dome at the top. The edifice was to rest on a small square plinth, and thus be seen to rise dramatically from the landscape at the top of the hill. However, instead of the proposed arcade Carlisle — with Bramante's Tempietto at San Pietro in Montorio in mind — requested a colonnade, and Hawksmoor made the necessary alterations to the design, which had the effect of making the structure a taller one.

During the 1730s problems and revisions dogged the project and Hawksmoor found control of the project wrested away from him. Construction difficulties and ill health made matters worse for him, and even before his death he was yielding to arguments over the entablature, the spacing of the colonnade and the design of the upper storey. The final version included steps on the eastern side, fashioned like those at Lord Burlington's villa in Chiswick in London, and a bastion wall, added by Burlington's protegé Daniel Garrett in the early 1740s and completely destroying Hawksmoor's intended effect of the building thrusting out of the hilltop.

Nevertheless a stunning architectural landmark from wherever one spies it, the Mausoleum contains, above the vaults, a chapel lit by large windows and a clerestory some 70 feet/21 metres high. The eight fluted Corinthian columns inside echo the twenty Doric columns of the colonnade outside. Perhaps the ultimate confirmation of Carlisle's dynastic aspirations lies in the fact that the Mausoleum is still the burial place of the Howard family. Beneath the chapel is a crypt, with a central vaulted chamber linked to a circular passageway around the perimeter and four small chambers issuing from it, and catacombs that contain sixty-three loculi or niches, less than half of which are filled.

With so much water surrounding Castle Howard and all its buildings, there is always scope for a dramatic reflection somewhere in the landscape.

THE MAUSOLEUM

LEFT ABOVE Standing on the top of Mount Sion Hill, Hawksmoor's Mausoleum was begun in 1728 and completed after his death in the early 1740s, when Daniel Garrett built the bastion wall that surrounds the building.

LEFT BELOW For more than two centuries the Mausoleum has been the private burial place of the Howard family, eleven generations of whom have occupied Castle Howard since it was built.

BELOW The view from New River Bridge towards the Mausoleum.

Even on a dull day the distinct silhouette of the Mausoleum against the skyline ensures its dramatic presence in the landscape.

AUTUMN

Like spring, autumn is a season full of delights at Castle Howard. Individual trees and clumps of woodland all begin to change colour and shape as their leaves turn and fall. Autumn also presents heavy broody skies, which seem to accentuate the oranges and reds of the foliage.

ABOVE The West Wing, framed by overhanging branches.

RIGHT A silver birch standing beside the South Lake.

LEFT The statue of Apollo on his ornate pedestal makes an eye-catcher at the end of the Lime Walk.

ABOVE The view from New River Bridge towards the Waterfall. September sunlight and green foliage on the cusp of autumnal decay combine with the honey-coloured stone to produce a golden hue.

LEFT ABOVE Autumnal maple leaves in Ray Wood.

LEFT BELOW *Agrocybe rivulosa* is a relatively new fungi to arrive in the UK, usually found on wood-chip piles or nestling beneath trees. It has yet to acquire a common name.

BELOW LEFT Fallen leaves of all colours begin to carpet the lawns in autumn.

BELOW RIGHT More maple leaves in Ray Wood: these are *Acer palmatum* var. *heptalobum*.

ABOVE Modelled on William Kent's designs of 1733 for the Houses of Parliament,
Robinson's West Wing would make an impressive symmetrical front for any building.

RIGHT Fallen leaves gather on the eastern shore of the South Lake.

Birch trees overhanging the approach to the temple.

Sweet chestnut trees on the eastern boundary of the South Parterre.

THE ATLAS FOUNTAIN

The Atlas Fountain, together with the Prince of Wales Fountain, is part of the ornamental parterre to the south of the house, designed by the great Victorian landscape gardener William Andrews Nesfield in the mid-nineteenth century. A photograph taken in the 1870s (see page 22) reveals the intricate design of Nesfield's parterre, together with the dominant position of the Atlas Fountain, which was carved from Portland stone by the sculptor John Thomas, and weighed 24 tons. The fountain was fully refurbished in the 1980s.

When the water of the fountain begins to flow, the glassy surface of the water ripples, obscuring reflections, but the sight and sound of the jets add another dimension to this view.

As Atlas labours to support the world he is cooled by streams of
water blown through conch shells by each of the four tritons.

Nesfield's idea was for the sculptural complexity of the fountain
to complement the architectural richness of Vanbrugh's building.

LEFT Water, water everywhere: plumes of water rise from the top of the globe, tritons blow their streams over Atlas and smaller jets fill the lower scallop-shell basins.

BELOW Castle Howard is a landscape full of surprises. As one steps away from the fountain, the gigantic figures seem to shrink against the lime trees in the background. These were planted at the same time as the fountain was built.

Winter mist cloaks the house and the fountain lies dormant,
the basin having been drained during the cold weather.

WALLS AND GATES

Visitors approaching Castle Howard from the south leave the main A64 and wind their way up into the Howardian hills. There, at the southern extremity of the estate, they encounter the 7th Earl's Monument, which also marks the beginning of the famous Avenue that runs northwards in a straight line for 5 miles/8 kilometres. Flanked by plantings of beech and lime trees, the Avenue dips and rises to reveal a sequence of arches, turrets, pyramids, towers and eventually an obelisk at the head of the drive to the house. The Avenue marks the grandest of arrivals possible for eighteenth- and twenty-first-century visitors alike.

Clear skies and sunlight transform the Avenue into an extraordinary panorama. On arrival one passes first through the Carrmire Gate, and a mile later through the Gatehouse. Beyond stands the Obelisk.

ABOVE Rearing up from a stepped platform, the 7th Earl's Monument
marks one's entry to the Castle Howard estate.

RIGHT The column is crowned by a tripod that ends on curved swan necks,
which support a flaming brazier. On bright days the gilded superstructure
gleams in the sunlight and the top of the column is visible for miles around.
It takes on the appearance of a gigantic Roman candle.

OPPOSITE For visitors travelling to Castle Howard from the south the
Gatehouse is the third feature they encounter. It was originally designed as
a pyramid arch by Vanbrugh in 1718 and the wings were added in the 1750s.

WINTER

As the leaves fall and the days shorten, the first frosts arrive. In a cold winter the Great Lake and the South Lake freeze over. Dramatic winter sunsets fill the sky with wonderful colours, lending atmosphere to Castle Howard's Christmas festivities. As the estate is more than 330 feet/ 100 metres above sea level it is often blessed with a blanket of snow.

The yew hedges flanking the Atlas Fountain, topped with a light covering of snow; beyond, the house, shrouded in February mist. The fountain does not play in freezing weather.

BELOW Watery sunlight fails to dispel the winter fog.

CENTRE After the rich colours of spring, summer and autumn, in the depths of winter the landscape takes on a stark, monochrome quality.

FAR RIGHT February snowfall covers the ground but leaves the figure of Silenus unscathed.

December ice on the South Lake.

From this vantage point above Temple Hole Basin the change in water levels is apparent. The outflow from the South Lake drops 20 feet/6 metres into Temple Hole; at the far end the water cascades into New River via the Waterfall (its pinnacles visible in the middle distance), before flowing under the bridge and then dropping another 12 feet/3.5 metres. In the distance, on the summit of Mount Sion Hill, is Hawksmoor's Mausoleum.

LEFT A light fall of snow in December in front
of the house, seen from across the South Lake.

ABOVE Low winter sunlight leaves the fountain
and yew hedges in shadow.

CASTLE HOWARD

BELOW Castle Howard may be famous as a grand historic house that is
open to the public, but it is also a family home, and during December
visitors can enjoy its Christmas decorations indoors and outdoors.

RIGHT ABOVE As evening descends, lights shine out from inside the house.

RIGHT BELOW The great imposing presence of the dome means
it is impossible to confuse Castle Howard with any other house in the UK.
In the daytime the gilded lantern gleams in sunlight and at night
it is illuminated as a beacon visible for miles around.

FOLLOWING PAGES The December evening sky silhouettes the figure
of Bacchus, arm aloft, at the western end of the Temple Terrace.

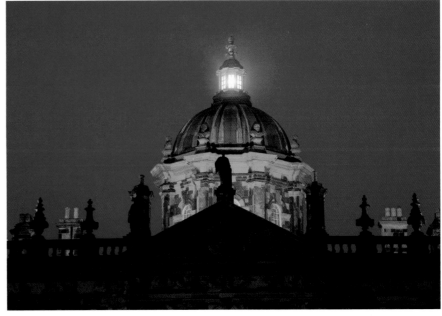

Photographer's notes

I had visited Castle Howard on several occasions and been commissioned to photograph the daffodils and rhododendrons, so I was already aware it was a very special place. But these were fleeting visits and when Castle Howard invited me to photograph the grounds over a whole season I knew this was to be a very extraordinary commission. I was given free access to the grounds, and I started photography in March, when the daffodils bloomed, and finished the following February, when the snowdrops were out. I returned later that July to do more photography in the Rose Gardens. That summer was one of the best flowerings the Rose Gardens had had for years.

As all photographers will know, the best light is very early in the morning, so I did much of the photography before the grounds were open to the public. I had only the peacocks and pheasants for company, reminding me of their presence with their haunting calls. Once I heard children laughing in the distance as the Howard family exercised their dogs, but I never saw them. This early photography, together with early evening photography, allowed me to photograph the landscape without people present and gave me an impression of what this estate must have been like when it was simply a family home as distinct from a national visitor attraction.

Overall I made many visits, trying to catch the right light in the right season. A memorable occasion was when I photographed the north façade of the house across the Dairy Pond. This was a must-have shot which had to be taken at 8.30 p.m. in June with the light on the house; I wanted the house reflecting in the still water. Several times I tried, but evening breezes rippled the pond each time. After four attempts I was about to give up and pack my gear away when the wind dropped, the water went still, the reflection appeared and as a bonus a black swan swam by. Magic.

I used Canon 1DSmk3 and Mamiya 645 AFD2 cameras. All images were shot digitally in raw file format. I used a tripod and cable release. As a photographer my objective is to always get the image right in camera, so I used neutral density graduated filters to balance the light and a polarizing filter to the enhance colour saturation, particularly of the plants and flowers. The raw files were processed in Adobe Lightroom and Photoshop and the only enhancements were to adjust colour balance and density.

My brief was simple: to show that the Castle Howard estate is a place worth visiting at any time of the year. I hope I have proved that it is.

Acknowledgements

Mike Kipling and Christopher Ridgway are grateful to Rachel Jack, Brian Deighton (head gardener) and Nick Cooke (head forester) at Castle Howard for their help with this book.

Index

Page numbers in *italic* refer to illustrations